"Lovebirds"

We now peer at the animalia kingdom,

the heralding in of the lovebird,

the agapornis as it is fancied,

these birds of passionate emotion are origin
of the African continent,

where eight of nine species reside there,

love birds are characterized by their
physique,

but I'm assuming they derive their name
from the fact that they're constantly in pair,

long live love everlasting I say,

long live.

"The cockatiels"

Its g'day to the cockatiels,

these blue web-footed birds derive from the Australian forests,

O , what wonder,

a cross between the sloth and seagull if you stare intently,

these Australian birds stand out,

just their footing does,

appearance is key with such particular birds,

O, cockatiels.

"Parrot"

Our first informative source,

tamed and trained in some cases,

to divulge earth's mysterious secrets,

is the parrot,

another class belonging to the aves,

a colorful bird with a conversation enough
to bring understanding that animals just
don't talk as we do still,

therefore,

no point in conversation really,

walk the talk, psittacine.

"Flamingo"

The world stands captivated by the flamingo
and it's flock gathered in the midst of
waters,

it's more so when they soar off unanimously
from where they once were,

just only four species of these indigenous
birds and there you have it,

the flamingoes,

pink pigmentation that makes them apart

from the ordinary,

flamingoes,

cheers to you.

"The cranes"

The class of aves,

it's the birds we've all positioned ourselves to when watching " The karate kid",

but this time,

these cranes,

specially and intricately created as they are,

their habitations are located on all corners of the globe, excluding the arctic and South America, some take flight while others are stationary,

take a kick at that,

cousins to the heron,

never barren are they,

the more,

the merrier.

"Firecrest"

This is,

the kinglet family

a bird stemming from harmonies with a song in itself,

the common firecrest,

not so common,

a relative to the gold crest bird,

a uniquely labelled fowl with a range of distance the size of most of what is western Europe,

"Regulus ignicapilla" as it goes,

also, "king of birds" as it is coined

across the atlantic,

what beautiful fantastic specimens.

"Penguins"

The vibrating waddle of the arctic penguins,

these peculiar fowls are just apiece of the bountiful view of the world and the deep amidst us,

peaceful and welcoming as they are,

the penguins engage in a ceremony of togetherness,

despite the chill.

"Air"

Without it,

we wouldn't be around for any such reason,

the air,

one of the main necessities propelling life,

one of them,

a major foundation for inhalation,

both lungs and air unite to service our
existence here,

unpolluted air is extremely essential and
must be attended to, and to make matters
extend,

take aim at the reaching for the stars, passed
midair,

beyond yonder way,

mine air,

just enough for me.

"Mist"

This may be somewhat hard in terms of explanation,

but it ought to be expounded,

as water in midair,

so is the formation of mist,

what we all call,

mist in the climate and zone its in,

this phenomena in which the nucleation sites occur,

there's no mystic in its presence.

"Herbs"

The vast of its essential uses,

such savory along with the aromatic in

contribution, herbs,

grateful for their existence,

the roles of life catering the best of its
offering to our need,

gentle,

yet powerful,

remedies from nature's heart to us all.

"Botanical gardens"

Eden again and probably so,

this organized collection of plantae exhibits
all that's lush and green for those seeking
the serene,

get a load of all of this ,

its ancient, present, and future combined,

the botanical gardens,

collected beauty from every corner.

"Banyan tree"

The furniture to the safari,

this tree,

sets itself as a standard of the tribal facade,

as you see it,

the study of the moraceae,

intro to life here on the continent,

good with all that's photogenic,

it's already positioned,

a more ethnic looking tree than others

is the banyan.

"Poppies"

In comes the papaveraceae,

better known as the poppy,

you pluck it in certain destinations,

you wind up sentenced,

distinct from the other kinds of flower,

lights up that particular place you see,

the poppies,

looks as though a population of them as
they are placed about the way,

as if they were,

the poppies,

ever decorative.

"Hurricane"

A major storm,

in a major way,

what're constructed things,

or a foundation to one of these?

arising in the day,

brewing as it may,

gathering itself into a havoc unstoppable,

like an unleashed temperament finally able
to be expressed,

this is the hurricane,

one of nature's emotions,

the hurricane,

nature intensified.

"Seasons"

The year,

divided into parts,

one for you,

and one for you,

and you,

then me,

satisfactory doesn't have neither role nor
say in this,

from the extreme sun beating down,

to the frost biting cold,

the seasons in hostile manner,

even wild are the times in which the years
within start to change,

survival it is.

"Peacock"

Decorative,

especially for a throne room.

the peacock,

unable to be eaten by ordinary man,

this fowl has a meaning of watchfulness,

along with other high traits in following
under its wings,

it's diverse colors expound beyond its own
life,

this is the pea,

to be admired.

"The toucan"

Enter the dense tropics where miraculous and sensation are hand in hand,

the bird significant to this introduction is the toucan,

a tribal symbol of showmanship,

so,

yes you can,

noticeable,

the definition behind this specific fowl,

stand up and be heard,

make yourself to be known,

and on the other hand,

take a dive into paradise.

"Butterflies"

Birth of beauty,

where it's at for blossoming love,

in the stomach is the starter,

and officially the way and sign for love from
ever being shown,

butterflies,

passions that never die,

multicolor are they,

these butterflies,

not so high they fly,

neither low,

but just enough to consider them level,

touch nature's utterance.

"Dandelions"

The only flower in the family species to fly away from its base after a single blow,

bliss,

what it looks like by this certain flower, we all want the real name to this piece of nature,

"Taraxacum" officially,

for common label,

initially for faithfulness , meaning by which its known forever,

yes indeed,

by its unanimous name,

thus,

Taraxacum.

"Snow"

Cold as we all know,

the result of what's no longer fluid,

or just snow as it is,

coated thoroughly atop the majestic
mountain tops just as vast as they are too,

such places,

white indeed, with no other color,

but it leaves room to imagine,

when all flee its presence or brace for it,

snow,

fierce,

but easily receding,

this is as far as it gets.

"Rainbow"

An insignia,

or better yet,

a sign of peace and never again of a
worldwide catastrophe engulfing the world
we live in,

a promise still,

a rainbow still,

the rich colors,

ordained to remain in their own lanes,

a good sign,

well indeed,

tis the rainbow as you know of it today,

no secrets to it,

all blatant,

a message in a bend.

"Clouds"

The heaven's entry way,

earth's expressive way of saying, "aloft",

clouds,

never strange,

just stationary,

at times,

clouds,

the sky's attachment,

making and forming images so grand,

creating imagination,

just these simple stores of precipitation,

yet still contain much weather,

lightly powerful.

"Ocean"

The deep has it,

jewels and the choir beneath chiming day
and night,

treasures from below,

it roars just like the lion,

an army of waters just as strong as the solid
ground

this is the ocean,

a mighty depth.

"Fireflies"

Wow,

the lighting up from these insects alone,

the sensational beauty to them,

decorative living things only by night
mainly,

like stars stationed above,

only these as much,

like comets soaring through and about the
atmosphere,

yet in best of climate,

they know when to light it up,

nature's lanterns,

see the night.

"Sand"

Every grain of sand,

the earth's result from rock,

sand as it is,

has it's own portrait,

the dunes preach the aftermath of a climb
to the top,

and the sands of time are closing in,

lesson from this observance,

every grain,

elaborate much,

depicts how far and vast the world around
has gone,

shall I count each one,

only time will tell,

sands,

one body yet within,

much.

"Mountains"

Extraordinaire,

high up are the earth's rocky majestic faces,

yes indeed the earth is told in many ways,

carrying many faces,

these are firm,

these are the ground power ascending
upward,

the penetrable force due to what ascending
up because of what occurred earlier,

mountains,

if you look on from top downward,

you can imagine the soar,

but the mountains,

how and what it all means to be elevated.

"Lily pads"

These are the creativity of one of the world's expressive phenomena,

if only I could stand on them just as I do on ground where I am,

lily pads,

as they are named,

the earth's beauties since the formation of existence,

the nuphar and victoria amazonica,

although light,

heavy and dense with gentle firmness,

eloquent,

with much to expound on.

"Morning"

The sun and blue both to bring you about
what's called day,

this is the theory,

no theory,

birth begins from horizons,

and the day's mouth opens to bring life a
respectful awakening,

nothing abrupt,

this is the time,

the hours that aren't surprised,

this is the a.m.

and it's good.

"Rocks"

That's what they're made for,

that purpose, to crush,

but also, can be too,

rocks,

have their own grouping,

not just rocks just to be there,

every kind has its own address and story on
how it came about,

the explanation of rocks is this,

life as well all know and comprehend,

made them hard,

they're formed from the aftermath of what

was once fluid and heated,

yet special,

earth's history.

"Fir trees"

Winter season messaged all over this plant,

this tree,

distinctive from others in such a way,

far from dismay

when you see these trees,

tis the season,

and jolly comes to mind,

fir trees,

pinaceae family,

related to cedar to root,

found all around.

"Lightning"

Crackling across the night sky,

it speaks for itself,

what was once used to translate God's wrath,

is no more than aspects of the sky's system of saying, " It's part of me"

yea, and every time it makes that statement, to me,

I see a form of different sky,

it's the sky's expression written all over,

light in the night just goes to tell,

that the light overall,

exceeds indeed.

"Volcanoes"
Not just a mountain,
deep within,
from the top down,
intensified heat beyond fires strength,
these are earth's canons,
beware the brink of it,
every part of nature has its own expressions.

"Blossoms"
Flourishing flowers,
and the entire set,
it ascends straight into the atmosphere
alongside others,

grow,

sprout,

grow as the sun assists,

those irresistible blossoms,

the lessons in this life,

blossoms,

probably not the grandest of introductions

but that's how us folk germinate ourselves,

starts off by seed.

"Nature's course"

Not of any course,

but here's what it is,

That wild side and tendency to thrill

whether it engages itself or not,

the rage,

the crash,

the beat down of rain and hail,

thunder and storm,

It's all a raging network without limits,

tumultuous,

but it's temporary,

only for a season,

then the calm will preside;

and all the works of the heavens

will continue as ever before.

"The wild"

The Rhino charging,

and the ram too,

at war,

yet the bird is high up in the trees,

from the Americas to the savannah,

It's all wild and rich,

an unspeaking beauty;

the honey bees to the watering holes

all of it is a wild connection,

the wild will always be.

"Cascades"

Throat to the earth's system,

this is awesome,

this is breathtaking,

amazing sight,

If you peer close enough,

the more attention spent on such magnificent beauty,

just a glimpse of these cascades, a yearning of power,

If not that,

a lesson of success,

then is the wellspring, from which these cascades originate,

connect with such beauty,

goes to show more beauty than catastrophe.

"Sky"

Canopy of the world,

but it's not a wrap although,

'til the sky is over,

and when it sets over,

gaze at wonder,

gaze and wander,

the distance from ground level,

O, sky,

how all had tried to reach you,

you the unreachable,

all but the limit,

above air,

placed to reign,

governs and surveys all that is beneath.

"Waves"

Crashing down,

crashing over,

Wading it out,

emotion,

the waves,

a sort of essence that its own toll can't fully
express,

so, powerful and beyond what words and
imagination can express,

well,

to see it all,

ride it on.

"Seed"
Prior to its germination,
birth,
beginning of all life and growth,
It starts off like so,
a simple seed deep in the soft and breakable

soil,

start of whatever is to go beyond the ovule,

a lesson,

an application on humans,

here on what we have called home,

when life comes from out of the opening,

where all is born.

"Mangroves"

These dense, natural gatherings of life,

all clustered together near swamp area,

halophytes,

as they're referred to,

work with low level places on this earth,

mainly mud,

which are attractive in most cases,

thrive and lively faces,

letting you know your entry way to paradise,

to nature's advances,

purely, a tour of energy without waste,

indeed,

mangroves,

epitome of the biome,

so far, so good.

"Ants"

Nature's unseen employees,

striving daily to come up with their means,

this just means,

that their unlike grotesque sizes,

contain massive amount of duty,

ants,

tiny tools to the world we're in,

lessons from the smallest in count,

surmounts to the moral of the story,

the more,

the merrier.

"Star fish"

Introducing,

the echinoderm,

residing deep in the depths of the seas,

making the most of the beneath and its degrees,

It's attractive shape beckons speculation,

sensitive at the touch,

retaliates by shutting itself off from all things,

this time,

no wish made,

only the star fish,

not ever denoting to gills,

both above surface and underneath,

they are alive to make folks surprised when spotted.

it's all eyes.

"Nest"

Circular composition is this station,

braced and made to prevent from endangering occurrences,

the nest,

epicenter of beginning life,

the notion we all take into understanding as

baby steps,

from ostriches to various species of bird,

the nest is a symbol of base,

whether high up, or eye level,

is where these fabulous creations are located,

never to be touched or else abandoned,

are these delicate nests,

remember home the young age,

and the times you ventured from it,

now,

farewell after grown.

"Anemones"

These living organisms,

situated below,

are the absorbents of the deep?

ambassadors of both sea beneath and
mysteries unknown down in the depths of
the ocean,

motionless are they by far,

swaying alongside the current underneath,

taking on prey,

to further exist,

hideous do they may seem by peer,

but phenomenal as they appear,

such as these,

apart from others.

"The clam"

Now,

speaking of jewelry,

the clam,

it's origin by pearl,

these specimens,

agents of shine and from within,

rare,

beware their expense,

the pearl that's in,

nestled,

positioned in the mid-section of the clam,

saying "a just of who I am,"

these organisms,

are the decorative of the sea down beneath,

and never to be underestimated,

to the clam,

I say,
riches,
all natural.

"Aloe"
All natural,
and nature's balm,
one of them,
created to serve,
and shouldn't be mistreated,
faster grown when heated,
originally placed in tropical zones,
a leisure may it be,
to have something

to own,

aloe,

blessed and nature's product.

"Moon"

Deep craters,

catering to more discovery,

the moon and its shine in cooperation

to earth,

sister to our planet,

a couple's night picnic speculation,

this is the moon that faces us every night,

looks like a moment away,

yet,

repeatedly so is it ever far off,

governor of nightfall,

where the strength of gravitational pull is,

bliss,

all said,

to the moon and back.

"Coral reef"

Architect of the deep below,

and more in row,

how exquisite the sight of what's
underneath?

no enchantments,

strictly the pearls of nature,

I'd coin,

these are the coral reefs;

he that beheld face invites us to discover,

how about we all join?

" The gecko"

The coolest reptile amongst them,

slender, quick,

kingdom Animalia,

of the squamation order,

already makings its way to our domain,

adaptive to much heated of climates,

known to chirp to other geckos,

indeed, it derives its name from the Malay
language,

for its unique sound in making,

the gecko,

on some serious hype these creatures are;

venture into the world of the gecko,

discover while raising the bar.

Acknowledgement

In humble regards to God's abundant creation of life:

"But ask the animals, and they will teach you,

    or the birds in the sky, and they will tell

you;

or speak to the earth, and it will teach you,

or let the fish in the sea inform you.

Which of all these does not know

that the hand of the Lord has done this?

In His hand is the life of every creature

and the breath of all mankind." Job 12: 7-10

www.ingramcontent.com/pod-product-compliance
Lightning Source LLC
Chambersburg PA
CBHW020904310526
45786CB00018B/1745